EXECUTIVE EDITORS
Mike Mifsud, Alan Doan, Jenny Doan,
Sarah Galbraith, David Mifsud

MANAGING EDITOR
Natalie Earnheart

CREATIVE DIRECTOR
Christine Ricks

PHOTOGRAPHY TEAM
Mike Brunner, Lauren Dorton, Jennifer Dowling,
Dustin Weant

PATTERN TEAM
Edie McGinnis, Denise Lane, Jessica Woods,
Gregg Allnutt

PROJECT DESIGN TEAM
Jenny Doan, Natalie Earnheart, Janet Yamamoto

EDITOR & COPYWRITERS
Jenny Doan, Natalie Earnheart, Christine Ricks,
Katie Mifsud, Camille Maddox, Nichole Spravzoff,
Edie McGinnis

SEWIST TEAM
Jenny Doan, Natalie Earnheart, Janet Yamamoto,
Carol Henderson, Denise Lane, Janice Richardson,
Jamey Stone

QUILTING & BINDING DEPARTMENT
Sarah Richardson, Betty Bates, Karla Zinkand,
Natalie Loucks, Debbie Elder, Jan Meek, Angela
Wilson, Chelsea White, Mary McPhee, Charlene
McCabe, Dennis Voss, Debbie Allen, Jamee Gilgour,
Michelle Templeton, Frank Jones, Kara Snow, Ethan
Lucas, Devin Ragle, Bruce VanIperen, Lyndia Lovell,
Aaron Crawford, Cyera Cottrill, Deborah Warner,
Salena Smiley, Francesca Flemming, Rachael Joyce,
Bernice Kelly, Deloris Burnett

PRINTING COORDINATORS
Rob Stoebener, Seann Dwyer

PRINTING SERVICES
Walsworth Print Group
803 South Missouri
Marceline, MO 64658

CONTACT US
Missouri Star Quilt Company
114 N Davis
Hamilton, Mo. 64644
888-571-1122
info@missouriquiltco.com

content

Oops! Sometimes we make mistakes.
To find corrections to every issue of Block
go to: **www.msqc.co/corrections**

hello
from MSQC

Fall is my favorite season because it's the time of year that causes me to pause and take in the beauty all around me. It's a brilliant reminder to stop and smell the roses, or at least step out of my way to feel the satisfying crunch of a fallen leaf. Quilting is much the same. When I set aside at least a small part of my time and spend it making something useful and beautiful, it enriches the rest of my day.

When autumn breezes start to blow, I know it's time to curl up with a comfy quilt and enjoy a moment with the fruit of my labors. I may not have had a great harvest from my vegetable garden this year, but I did have a wonderful quilt harvest! There's so much to love about the fall. I love digging into my stockpile of sweaters, baking up pies from the last of the season's fruit, stoking the fire, and gathering my family around me to celebrate all we have to be grateful for.

This fall, I wish you the best of the season, from the taste of a tart, ripe apple to the warm embrace of a cozy quilt. Take time to enjoy everything that makes this time of year special and give yourself the freedom to let the leaves pile up while you do a little stitching. Then, when you're all through, go ahead and jump right in!

Jenny

JENNY DOAN
MISSOURI STAR QUILT CO

TRY OUR APP

It's easy to keep up on every issue of BLOCK magazine. Access it from all your devices. And when you subscribe to BLOCK, it's free with your subscription! For the app search BLOCK magazine in the app store. Available for both Apple and Android.

follow
the sun

The leaves are beginning to change around here. I love when the air gets a little nippy and I can pull out my jacket or sweater to go outside. I've noticed recently that we have a lot of sunflowers growing around my house. I'm not sure how they got there but they've been so lovely lingering in the slightly cooler weather. I like to watch their heads turn and follow the sun throughout the day. Their sunny, yellow faces remind me to overlook small challenges and seek out opportunities to appreciate all the wonderful things that are constant in my life.

Quilting is one of those wonderful things. It calls my attention back to doing things for others and I enjoy putting love into that process. I know many of my quilting friends have had their homes and lives recently devastated by natural disasters. In that moment of tragedy I've witnessed a loving community of quilters reach out to them. Their sunny faces are also why I love this work so much. Thank you, dear quilters, for being the sunshine in such challenging times. You make the world a better place!

CHRISTINE RICKS
MSQC Creative Director, BLOCK MAGAZINE

PRINTS

FBY57907 Yes, Please - Main Cream Metallic by Jen Allyson for Riley Blake
SKU: SC6550-CREAM

FBY54387 Shades of the Season 10 - Sunflowers Metallic Yardage by Studio RK for Robert Kaufman
SKU: 20555 19

FBY57406 Bee Basics - Gingham Orange Yardage by Lori Holt for Riley Blake
SKU: C6400-ORANGE

FBY47576 Chatterbox Aprons - Chatterbox Gingham Blue by Mary Mulari for Penny Rose Fabrics
SKU: C5464-BLUE

FBY54414 Autumn Road - Tiny Flowers Orange by Katie Doucette for Wilmington Prints
SKU: Q1897-54535-852

FBY58257 Big Sky - Montana Azure Yardage by Annie Brady for Moda Fabrics
SKU: 16700 14

SOLIDS

FBY9016 Grunge Basics - Cream by BasicGrey for Moda
SKU: 30150 160

FBY45238 Grunge Basics - Lemon Drop by BasicGrey for Moda
SKU: 30150 321

FBY57811 Grunge Basics - Cantalope by BasicGrey for Moda
SKU: 30150 424

FBY14685 Grunge Basics - Sky Blue by BasicGrey for Moda
SKU: 30150 218

FBY57809 Grunge Basics - Butterscotch by BasicGrey for Moda
SKU: 30150 421

FBY14691 Grunge Basics - Peacock by BasicGrey for Moda
SKU: 30150 230

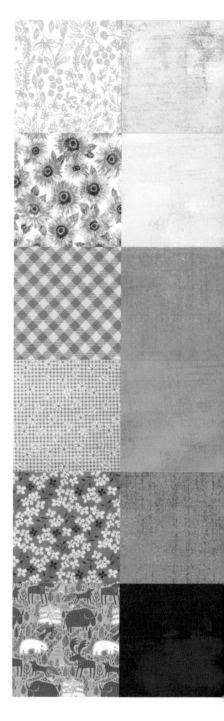

disappearing pinwheel twist

Our little town of Hamilton, Missouri, is a quiet place. We have just one traffic light and one little grocery store. There isn't a movie theater or shopping mall, but we do have acres and acres of beautiful farmland and a quaint, old-fashioned downtown. And everywhere you go, you're sure to bump into someone you've known since grade school.

Life in a small town has a pace of its own; seasons are marked with traditions that bring the community together: summertime movies in the park, the lighting of the Christmas display in early winter, and, perhaps most important of all, Friday night football in the fall.

If you visit Hamilton on game night, you're sure to find the streets empty. No one is out shopping or running errands because the whole town is gathered in the stands of the Penney High football stadium. After all, when you live in a small town, football is everything!

For the tutorial and everything you need to make this quilt visit:
www.msqc.co/blockfall17

disappearing pinwheel twist quilt

We are lucky to have a team that is quite good; our boys have won the state championship four times, so we wear our navy blue and gold with pride. Signs and slogans can be found all across town, and Hornet flags hang from the light poles.

Before a game, everyone arrives early to grab a pork burger and get a good seat. By opening kickoff, the stadium is packed and latecomers line the sidelines. Our fans are fiercely loyal, and we've developed a few superstitious traditions to ensure

a good game. One gal passes around "good luck" chocolate chip cookies, the football players' moms wear matching t-shirts, and the cheerleaders spend hours painting banners for the football players to run through. All in all, it makes for a wonderful night under those bright stadium lights.

This year we have a grandson on the team, a cheerleading granddaughter, and another granddaughter who plays in the band, so more than ever, there's nowhere I'd rather spend a Friday night than at the game. Go Hornets!

materials

QUILT SIZE
81" x 99"

BLOCK SIZE
11" x 12" finished

QUILT TOP
1 package print 10" squares
1 package background 10" squares

INNER BORDER
¾ yard

OUTER BORDER
1¾ yards

BINDING
¾ yard

BACKING
2½ yards 108" wide

SAMPLE QUILT
Shibori II by Debbie Maddy of Tiori
Designs for Moda Fabrics

1 block construction

Layer a background 10" square with a print 10" square. Sew all the way around the perimeter, using a ¼" seam allowance. Cut the square from corner to corner twice on the diagonal to **make 4** half-square triangles. Open the triangles and press toward the darkest color. Trim each half-square triangle to 6½". **1A**

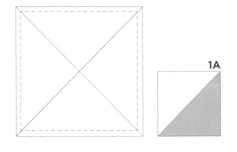

Sew 4 half-square triangles together as shown to make a pinwheel. **Make 42**. **1B**

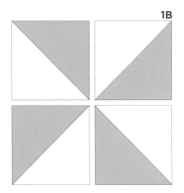

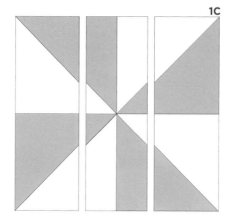

1C

Line up a rotary cutting ruler on the center seam line. Cut 2⅛" from the seam on both vertical sides of the line with a rotary cutter. 1C

Trade the piece that is on the left with the one on the right. 1D

Sew the 3 rows together to complete the block. Notice that it is a rectangle rather than a square. **Make 42** blocks. 1E

Block Size: 11" x 12" finished

2 arrange and sew

Sew the blocks together in rows of 6. Press the seam allowances of the odd rows toward the right and the even rows toward the left to make the seams "nest." **Make 7** rows and sew the rows together.

3 inner border

Cut (8) 2½" strips across the width of fabric. Sew the strips together end-to-end to make one long strip. Trim the borders from this strip.

Refer to Borders (pg. 111) in the Construction Basics to measure and cut the inner borders. The strips are approximately 84½" for the sides and approximately 70½" for the top and bottom.

4 outer border

Cut (9) 6" strips across the width of the fabric. Sew the strips together end-to-end to make one long strip. Trim the borders from this strip.

Refer to Borders (pg. 111) in the Construction Basics to measure and cut the outer borders. The strips are approximately 88½" for the sides and approximately 81½" for the top and bottom.

5 quilt and bind

Layer the quilt with batting and backing and quilt. After the quilting is complete, square up the quilt and trim away all excess batting and backing. Add binding to complete the quilt. See Construction Basics (pg. 111) for binding instructions.

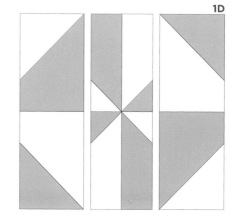

1D

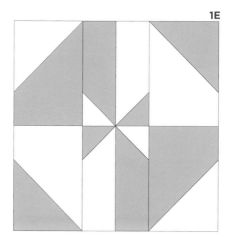

1E

1 Layer a print 10″ square with a white 10″ square with right sides facing. Sew all the way around the perimeter, then cut the sewn squares from corner to corner twice on the diagonal.

2 Open each half-square triangle unit and press the seam allowance toward the darker fabric. Square each to 6½″.

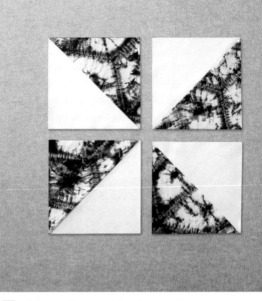

3 Sew 4 half-square triangles together as shown to make a pinwheel.

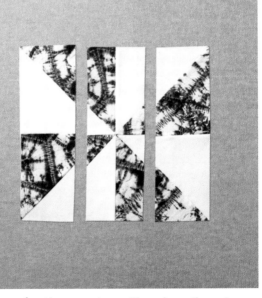

4 Line up a rotary cutting ruler on the center seam line. Cut 2⅛″ from the seam on both vertical sides of the seam with a rotary cutter.

5 Trade the piece that is on the left with the one on the right.

6 Sew the 3 rows together to complete the block. Notice the block is rectangular rather than square.

grand adventures

Life is a grand adventure. I'm the kind of person who loves surprises, and I love waking up every day, wondering what might take place out of the ordinary. When the lights go out during a thunderstorm, I can't wait to grab the candles, cozy up with a quilt, and play some board games. I like to say we have the best storms here in Missouri. When the thunder starts booming and the sky gets dark, you can bet you'll find us out on the front porch watching the clouds roll in.

Back in California, when the ground would rumble a little, we thought nothing of minor earthquakes and would go about our daily business. When we came to Missouri and heard about the tornadoes I thought, "Dorothy, we're not in Kansas anymore!" The idea of hiding in a cellar until a tornado passed terrified us, but the locals were unfazed. They told us, "How could you live where there are earthquakes? We just have big storms here." We have since learned to be in awe of Mother Nature and try to be as prepared as we can be. Now we sit back and enjoy the show.

For the tutorial and everything you need to make this quilt visit:
www.msqc.co/blockfall17

It doesn't happen all that often, but a couple of times a year we get a really good storm. It happened right in the middle of a retreat at the Sewing Center, and quilters were stitching away at their machines when the tornado siren went off. So, down into the storm cellar everyone went. I called in to ask how everyone was doing. Of course they were well looked after and perfectly safe, but some of our guests were feeling a bit scared. Well, I knew just the thing to do!

I took my cue from Julie Andrews in *The Sound of Music*, jumped in my car, and drove over to the Sewing Center where I promptly started singing "My Favorite Things"

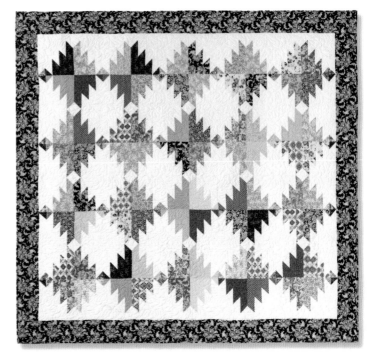

while twirling and dancing around. Everyone got a good laugh out of my impromptu performance and thankfully the storm passed without incident. Now don't let our weather stop you from coming to a retreat out here with us. We promise we'll take good care of you and we'd never let you blow away in a storm! You may even get a performance from yours truly!

The next time you find yourself troubled, remember that the answer is found in these simple words: "When the dog bites. When the bee stings. When I'm feeling sad. I simply remember my favorite things and then I don't feel so bad!" I have always found that with a little humor and a lot of gratitude you can get through almost anything.

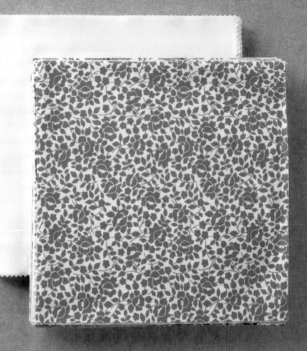

materials

QUILT SIZE
90¾" x 87¾"

BLOCK SIZE
15" x 18" finished

QUILT TOP
1 package 10" print squares
1 package 10" background squares

BORDER
¾ yard

OUTER BORDER
1¾ yards

BINDING
1 yard

BACKING
2¾ yards 108" wide

SAMPLE QUILT
Charming by Gerri Robinson of Planted
Seed Designs for Penny Rose Fabrics

1 mark, layer and sew

On 40 background squares, mark a
line from corner to corner once on the
diagonal. Layer the marked square with
a print square with right sides facing and
sew on either side of the drawn line. Cut
on the drawn line. Open each half-square
triangle and press the seam allowance
toward the darker fabric. Square the
block to 9½". **1A**

Stack 40 half-square triangles with the
center seam going from lower right to
upper left. **1B**

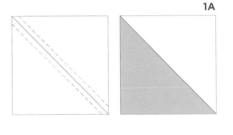

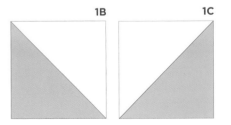

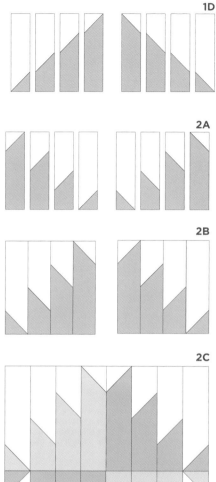

1D

2A

2B

2C

4A

4B

Stack the remaining half-square triangles so the center seam is going from lower left to upper right. 1C

Cut each half-square triangle into (4) 2⅜" strips. 1D

2 trading places

Trade the two outer strips with each other, then trade the two inside strips. 2A

Sew the strips together to make one quadrant of the block. 2B

Sew 4 quadrants together as shown to make one complete block. **Make 20.** 2C

Block Size: 15" x 18" finished

3 arrange in rows

Lay out the blocks in rows. Each row has 5 blocks across and there are 4 rows. Sew the blocks into rows, then sew the rows together to complete the top.

4 inner border

From the 2 remaining 10" print squares, cut (16) 2⅜" squares. Fold or mark each square from corner to corner once on the diagonal.

From the background fabric, cut:
- (8) 2⅜" strips across the width of the fabric. Subcut 1 strip into (4) 2⅜" x 9½" rectangles.

Subcut each of 3 strips into (2) 2⅜" x 18½" rectangles for a **total of 6**. Set the remaining strips aside for the top and bottom borders.

Place a print 2⅜" square atop a 2⅜" x 9½" rectangle with right sides facing. Sew on the marked line, then trim the excess fabric ¼" away from the sewn seam. **Make 2** with the marked line oriented from bottom right to upper left and 2 with the diagonal line oriented from bottom left to upper right as shown. 4A

Place a print 2⅜" square atop both ends of a 2⅜" x 18½" rectangle with right sides facing. Sew on the marked line, then trim the excess fabric ¼" away from the sewn seams. Repeat for the remaining 2⅜" x 18½" rectangles. 4B

Join 3 long rectangles together, then add a short rectangle to either end of the strip (make sure the snowballed corner of the short rectangle is butted up against the snowballed end of the longer strip). **Make 2** and sew one to either side of the quilt.

Join the remaining 2⅜" x width of fabric strips together and cut the top and bottom borders from this strip. It should be approximately 79¼" for both borders. Sew one to the top of the quilt and the other to the bottom. If necessary, refer to page 110 to learn how to measure and cut the border strips.

1 Make half-square triangles and stack 40 with the center seam going from lower right to upper left.

2 Stack the remaining half-square triangles so the center seam is going from lower left to upper right.

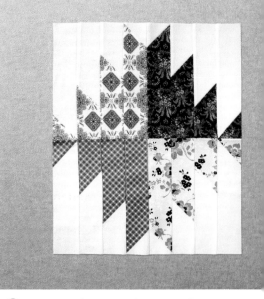

3 Cut each half-square triangle into (4) 2 ⅜" strips.

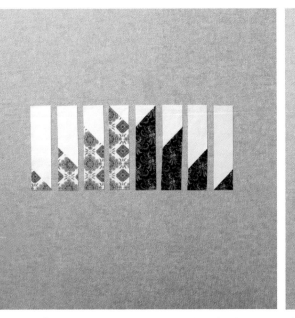

4 Trade the two outer strips with each other, then trade the two inside strips.

5 Sew the strips together to make one quadrant of the block.

6 Sew 4 quadrants together to complete the block.

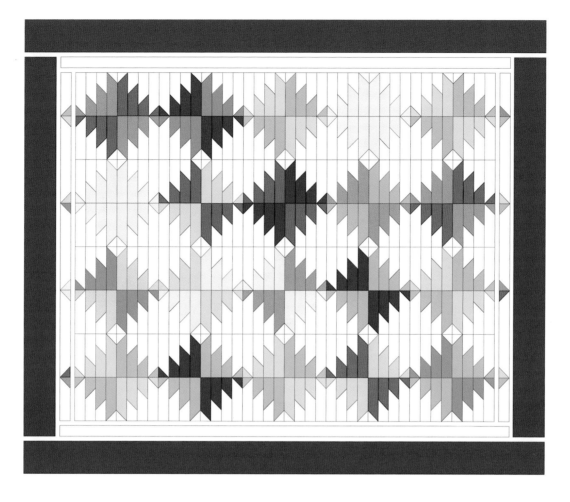

5 outer border

Cut (9) 6½" strips across the width of the fabric. Sew the strips together end-to-end to make one long strip. Trim the borders from this strip.

Refer to Borders (pg. 111) in the Construction Basics to measure and cut the outer borders. The strips are approximately 76¼" for the sides and approximately 91¼" for the top and bottom.

6 quilt and bind

Layer the quilt with batting and backing and quilt. After the quilting is complete, square up the quilt and trim away all excess batting and backing. Add binding to complete the quilt. See Construction Basics (pg. 111) for binding instructions.

herringbone quilt

For the tutorial and everything you need to make this quilt visit:
www.msqc.co/blockfall17

I love the thrill of the hunt. Whenever I get a free Saturday in the summertime, I'm off rummaging through garage sales for treasures to take home with me. And every time I spot a garage sale sign out of the corner of my eye, within a moment I've made a quick turn and I'm headed toward the sale, my heart thumping in anticipation. Going "garage saleing" is one of my favorite hobbies and who doesn't love a good bargain?

In the early years, when money was tight, anytime I needed something—from furniture to clothing—I went on a bargain hunt. Those were the days when my kids were growing out of their clothes like crazy. It was tough keeping them in pants that weren't high waders or ripped at the knees. Boy, those kids sure grew up fast!

One year, as summer was coming to an end and school was just around the corner, my daughter, Sarah, expressed a desire for Guess jeans. They were all the rage in their acid-washed glory with zippers at the back of the ankles and little bows at the top of the zippers. Those jeans were definitely cool and Sarah wanted to make a good impression on the first day of fourth grade. She begged and pleaded, but unfortunately, new school clothes weren't in the budget that year. I could tell she really had her heart set on those designer jeans and I wished that I could get them for her. In desperation, I told her to pray and ask God for them, and if God really wanted her to have Guess jeans, then

on Saturday when we went out "garage saleing" she just might find a pair.

Saturday arrived and all week Sarah had been eagerly awaiting our day of bargain hunting. Together we mapped out our route for the day; we were serious bargain hunters. As we walked out the front door to get in the van we noticed that our elderly neighbors across the street were having a garage sale. We debated whether or not to go check out the sale, imagining that it was filled with antique knickknacks, without a pair of jeans in sight. On a whim, Sarah said, "It can't hurt to look."

We headed across the street, not sure what we would find, and much to our surprise, they had a bunch of their grandchildren's clothes for sale. There, in the middle of the table, was a large pile of GUESS JEANS in Sarah's exact size! Sarah looked at me and said, "Mom, God wants me to have Guess jeans!" I laughed and replied that I supposed He did.

Maybe it was a silly thing to wish for, but it sure made her day. Finding those jeans was such a sweet lesson in hope for her and for the little girl in all of us! Sarah treasured those jeans and when they finally wore out, she carefully unstitched the little Guess logo and sewed them onto a new pair of jeans. Enjoy each happy little coincidence, dear quilters. I often find that they aren't coincidences at all.

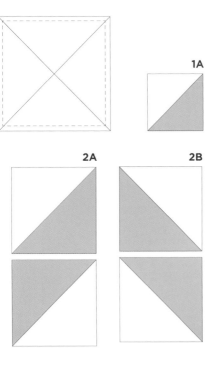

materials

QUILT SIZE
86" x 98"

BLOCK SIZE
6" x 12" finished

SUPPLIES
1 package 10" print squares
1 package 10" background squares

INNER BORDER
¾ yard

OUTER BORDER
1½ yards

BINDING
1 yard

BACKING
8 yards - horizontal seam(s)

SAMPLE QUILT
Safari Party by Melissa Mortenson
for Riley Blake Designs

1 make half-square triangles

Place a background 10" square atop a print 10" square with right sides facing. Sew all around the outer edge of the squares using a ¼" seam allowance.

Cut the sewn squares from corner to corner twice on the diagonal to **make 4** matching half-square triangle units. Open each half-square triangle and press the seam allowance toward the darker fabric. **1A**

Stack all matching half-square triangles together. You will have a total of 168

3A   **3B**

triangles. Square each half-square triangle unit to 6½".

2 sew

Block A

Sew 2 matching half-square triangles together as shown. **Make 42** and set aside for the moment. 2A

Block B

Sew 2 matching half-square triangles together as shown. Notice the direction is opposite that of Block A. **Make 36**. You should have 12 half-square triangles left. Set aside for the moment. 2B

Block Size: 6" x 12" finished

3 make vertical rows

Sew 7 A blocks together into a vertical row. Because we are using A blocks, we'll call these Row A. **Make 6** A rows. 3A

Sew 6 B blocks together into a vertical row. Add a half-square triangle to each end to complete the row. **Make 6** B rows. 3B

Sew the rows together alternating the A rows with the B rows. Refer to the diagram on page 31.

4 inner border

Cut (9) 2½" strips across the width of the fabric. Sew the strips together end-to-end to make one long strip. Trim the borders from this strip.

Refer to Borders (pg. 111) in the Construction Basics to measure and cut the inner borders. The strips are approximately 84½" for the sides and approximately 76½" for the top and bottom.

5 outer border

Cut (9) 5½" strips across the width of the fabric. Sew the strips together end-to-end to make one long strip. Trim the borders from this strip.

Refer to Borders (pg. 111) in the Construction Basics to measure and cut the outer borders. The strips are approximately 88½" for the sides and approximately 86½" for the top and bottom.

6 quilt and bind

Layer the quilt with batting and backing and quilt. After the quilting is complete, square up the quilt and trim away all excess batting and backing. Add binding to complete the quilt. See Construction Basics (pg. 111) for binding instructions.

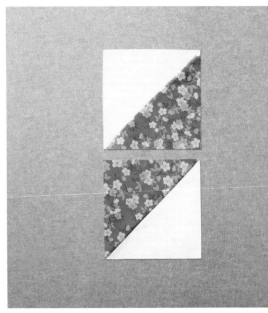

1 Place a 10″ background square atop a 10″ print square. Sew the squares together by sewing around the perimeter using a ¼″ seam allowance. Cut the sewn squares from corner to corner twice on the diagonal.

2 Open each half-square triangle unit and press the seam allowance toward the darker fabric. Trim each to 6½″.

3 Select 2 matching half-square triangles and sew them together as shown to make Block A. Notice the direction of the angle.

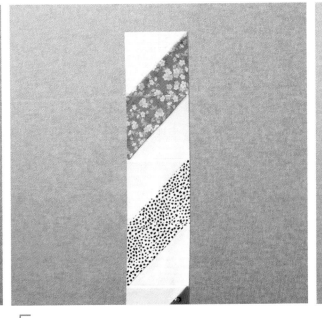

4 Select 2 matching half-square triangles and sew them together as shown to make Block B. The angle of the half-square triangles is opposite that of Block A.

5 Sew 7 A blocks together into a vertical row. Make 6 rows.

6 Sew 6 B blocks together into a vertical row. Add a half-square triangle unit to the top and the bottom to complete the row. Make 6.

pecking order

If you want your kids to develop lasting friendships with each other, play with them! Take a break from chores and schedules and all the busyness that comes with families, and make time to play! It doesn't have to be a perfectly planned event. No need to spend a bunch of money or travel to exciting locations. As long as you are together and free of distractions, a simple game of Uno will do the trick. Memories that last a lifetime are made around the game table, and if kids learn to have fun together when they're young, they're so much more likely to stay close as adults.

We have always loved playing as a family. When the kids were younger, we organized backyard baseball games and sang songs around the piano and walked to the park to feed the ducks. Now that the children are grown, I can truly say that they are friends.

These days, when the Doan family gets together, it's no small crowd. And with so many creative personalities in this bunch, there's always something exciting on the docket. We love games that we can all play together, from us old folks all the way down to the littlest grandkids. Of course, the competition isn't serious, but we sure have a lot of fun!

For the tutorial and everything you need to make this quilt visit:
www.msqc.co/blockfall17

One of our favorite things to do at game night is have a donut eating contest. Sounds easy, right? Well, this game has quite a twist: The donuts are dangling from strings, and you have to eat them without using your hands!

Prep is simple. All you need is one broom, two strings, and a box of donuts. The strings are tied to the handle of the broom and a donut is attached to the end of each string.

The game is played two contestants at a time. They lay down next to each other on the floor and the broom is held up so that the donuts hang just above their mouths. When the whistle is blown, it's a mad rush to devour every crumb of that donut! Of course, the donuts bob and swing with every tiny movement, so it can be tricky to grab a hold and take a bite.

The rest of the family crowds around and cheers as the players chomp at the air; it is always so funny to watch! By the end of the match, there is powdered sugar from heck to breakfast, and we are laughing so hard we can't breathe!

It's a simple thing, but I know my grandchildren will remember these times, and hopefully they'll still be "bobbing for donuts" for many years to come.

materials

QUILT SIZE
66" X 70½"

BLOCK SIZE
4½" finished

QUILT TOP
1 pack 5" solid squares
4 packs 5" print background squares

BORDER
1½ yards

BINDING
¾ yard

BACKING
4¼ yards – horizontal seam(s)

SAMPLE QUILT
Penned Pals by Ann Kelle for Robert Kaufman

1 cut

Cut each of 39 solid 5" squares in half vertically and horizontally to make (4) 2½" squares for a **total of 156.**

2 mark and sew

On the reverse side of the solid 2½" squares, draw a line from corner to corner once on the diagonal. **2A**

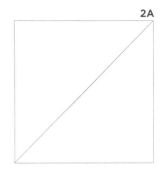

2B

Place a marked 2½" square on one corner of a 5" print background square. Sew on the line, then trim the excess fabric ¼" away from the sewn seam. Open and press the seam allowance toward the darker fabric to complete the block. **Make 156.** 2B

3 arrange and sew

Lay out the blocks in rows. Each row is made up of 12 blocks and 13 rows are needed. Refer to the diagram on page 39 and notice how each block is turned. After the blocks have been sewn into rows, press the seam allowances of the odd-numbered rows toward the right and the even-numbered rows toward the left to make the seams "nest."

Sew the rows together to complete the center of the quilt.

4 border

Cut (7) 6½" strips across the width of the fabric. Sew the strips together end-to-end to make one long strip. Trim the borders from this strip.

Refer to Borders (pg. 111) in the Construction Basics to measure and cut the outer borders. The strips are approximately 59" for the sides and approximately 66½" for the top and bottom.

5 quilt and bind

Layer the quilt with batting and backing and quilt. After the quilting is complete, square up the quilt and trim away all excess batting and backing. Add binding to complete the quilt. See Construction Basics (pg. 111) for binding instructions.

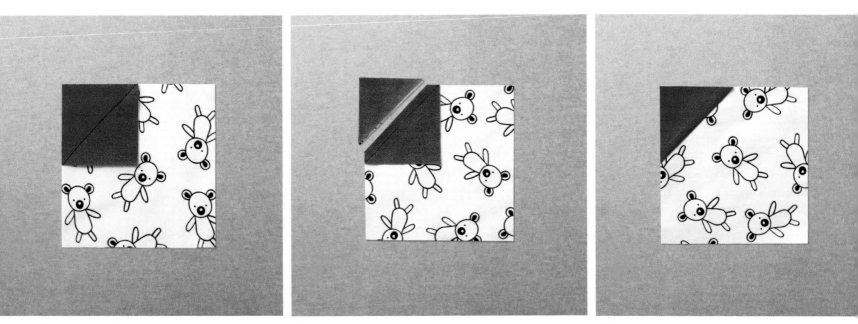

1 Mark a line from corner to corner once on the diagonal of a 2½″ background square and place it on 1 corner of a 5″ print square.

2 Sew on the marked line, then trim the excess fabric away ¼″ from the sewn seam.

3 Press the seam allowance toward the darker fabric to complete the block.

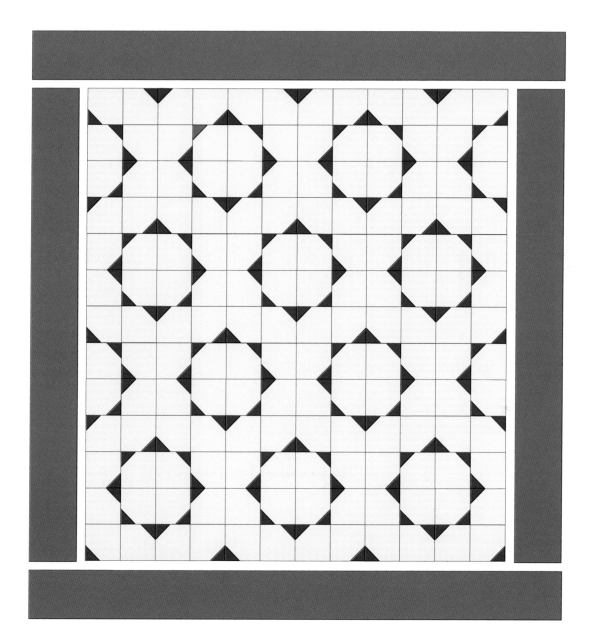

pony express

Some little girls dream of having a pony, but I wasn't one of those girls. We had a family dog, along with a bird, a horned toad, and even a chipmunk! My dad worked for Smuckers and when he went on business trips he would occasionally bring back a pet for me, which was an amazing surprise each time. I loved each pet and gave them names that corresponded to where my dad found them. For example, Alice, our bird, was from Alisal, California. Fidel, our dog, was from Castroville.

One of my best friends had a horse. Chipmunks and birds are one thing, but I had no experience with horses, except for Mr. Ed on television. She invited me to go riding with her and I felt a little unsure. The biggest animal I had was a dog and horses weren't exactly in my comfort zone. But she promised she would give me her most tame horse to ride, so I agreed.

That weekend we met up for a ride. The lettuce fields were her favorite place to ride and so off we went. My parents drove me and dropped me off in the fields not too far from the Spreckels Sugar Mill and my friend was waiting there with two horses. She showed me how to saddle and bridle my horse. It was intimidating being that close to such a large animal, but as I stroked his soft muzzle and smooth flank, I soon found myself mesmerized by this gentle giant.

For the tutorial and everything you need to make this quilt visit: **www.msqc.co/blockfall17**

After a couple of adjustments to the cinch and the stirrups, we were ready to ride. It took me a few tries to get up in the saddle, and gosh it was high up there! I got a quick lesson on how to stop and go. And that was it. I was on my own! All went well at first and if I pulled my reins to the left, he went left! I was finally starting to relax and really get into riding, feeling the loping stride of the horse beneath me and enjoying the scenery.

As a matter of fact, my confidence grew so quickly I thought I would try a trot. I gave my horse a little nudge with my heels and he quickly picked up the pace. It turns out trotting was A LOT of bouncing and bouncing and just when I thought I couldn't take the bouncing a minute more, the sprinklers in the field came on and spooked my gentle horse who took off like a shot. He began running for all he was worth and left me hanging on for dear life! All the lessons I had learned departed at that very moment and I couldn't remember to say whoa or to pull back on the reins. I was terrified. What had happened to my gentle giant?

Thankfully, my friend rode up alongside us and grabbed ahold of my reins, slowing my horse down again to a walk. Everything worked out in the end. I didn't die and neither did the horse, but the next day I could hardly walk—saddle sore, they called it. The next weekend she wanted to ride again and I wasn't ready just yet. But we did go riding a few more times and eventually I felt pretty comfortable on a horse, though it was always a couple hours before I could walk normally again.

materials

QUILT SIZE
83" X 83"

BLOCK SIZE
12" finished

QUILT TOP
1 package 10" print squares
4½ yards background fabric

BORDER
1½ yards

BINDING
¾ yard

BACKING
2¾ yards 108" wide fabric

SAMPLE QUILT
Chicken Scratch by Kaye England
for Wilmington Prints

1 cut

From the background fabric, cut:

- (4) 10" strips across the width of the fabric – subcut the strips into (4) 10" squares for a **total of 16.** Stack 13 of the 10" squares together to use when making half-square triangle units. Cut 2 of the remaining 10" squares into (8) 2½" x 4½" rectangles for a **total of 16.** Set aside for the moment. You will have (1) 10" square left over for another project.

- (15) 4½" strips across the width of the fabric – subcut 3 of the strips into (8) 4½" squares for a **total of 24.** Cut 1 strip into (1) 4½" square and stack it with the other squares of that size. Cut the remainder of the strip into (14) 2½" x 4½" rectangles. Cut the remaining 11 strips into 2½" x 4½" rectangles. Each strip will yield 16 rectangles. Add the 16 rectangles cut from the 10" squares to the stack for a **total of 206 rectangles.** There will be 6 rectangles left over.

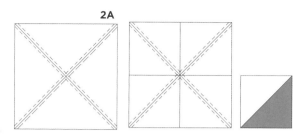

2A

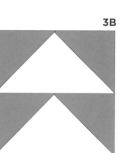

3A   3B

- (20) 2½" strips across the width of the fabric. Subcut each strip into (3) 2½" x 12½" rectangles for a **total of 60.** Set the strips aside for sashing.

From the 10" print squares:

- Select 28 squares. Cut each into (16) 2½" squares for a **total of 448.** Keep all matching prints stacked together. Set aside 36 squares to use as cornerstones in the sashing. There will be (12) 2½" squares left over for another project.

2 make half-square triangle units

On the reverse side of (13) 10" background squares, draw a line from corner to corner twice on the diagonal. Layer a marked background square with a 10" print square with right sides facing. Sew on both sides of the marked lines using a ¼" seam allowance. Cut each sewn square in half vertically and horizontally, then cut on the drawn lines. Each pair of sewn squares will yield 8 half-square triangles for a **total of 104.** Square up each half-square triangle unit to 4½". Set 4 half-square triangles aside for another project. 2A

3 block construction

Make 8 flying geese units. Select 16 matching 2½" print squares and (8) 2½" x 4½" background rectangles. Draw a line from corner to corner once on the diagonal on the reverse side of each print square. Place a marked 2½" square on 1 corner of a background rectangle. Sew on the marked line, then trim ¼" away from the sewn seam. Repeat for the adjacent corner of the rectangle to complete 1 flying geese unit. 3A

Sew 2 flying geese units together. **Make 4.** 3B

Sew a half-square triangle unit to either side of a flying geese strip. **Make 2 rows** in this manner. 3C

Sew a flying geese strip to 2 sides of a 4½" background square to make the center row of the block. 3D

Sew the three rows together as shown to complete 1 block. **Make 25 blocks.** 3E

Block Size: 12" Finished

4 arrange and sew

Lay out the blocks in 5 rows of 5 blocks. Add a 2½" x 12½" sashing rectangle at the beginning and end of each row and between each block. Press all seam allowances toward the blocks. 4A

Make horizontal sashing strips by sewing a 2½" cornerstone to a 12½" sashing rectangle.

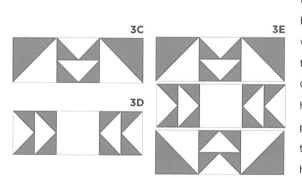

3C   3E

3D

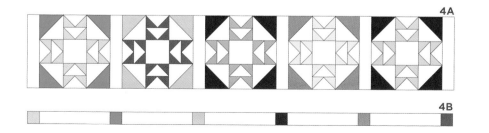

4A

4B

1 Draw a line from corner to corner twice on the reverse side of a background square. Layer it with a print square with right sides facing and sew on both sides of the lines. Cut in half vertically and horizontally, then cut on the drawn lines.

2 Make flying geese units. Sew a marked 2½″ print square to a background 2½″ x 4½″ rectangle with right sides facing. Sew on the marked line, then trim ¼″ away from the sewn seam. Repeat for the adjacent corner.

3 Sew 2 flying geese together. Make 4 matching units per block.

4 Sew a half-square triangle unit to either side of a flying geese unit to make the top and bottom row of the block.

5 Sew a flying geese unit to either side of a 4½″ background square to make the center row.

6 Sew the 3 rows together to complete the block.

Add a 2½" cornerstone, then another sashing rectangle. Continue in this manner until you have a strip consisting of 6 cornerstones and 5 rectangles. Press all seam allowances toward the cornerstones.
4B

Sew the rows of blocks together, adding a horizontal sashing strip between each row. After the rows have been sewn together, sew a sashing strip to the top and bottom to complete the center of the quilt top.

5 border

Cut (8) 6" strips across the width of the fabric. Sew the strips together end-to-end to make one long strip. Trim the borders from this strip.

Refer to Borders (pg. 111) in the Construction Basics to measure and cut the outer borders. The strips are approximately 72½" for the sides and approximately 83½" for the top and bottom.

6 quilt and bind

Layer the quilt with batting and backing and quilt. After the quilting is complete, square up the quilt and trim away all excess batting and backing. Add binding to complete the quilt. See Construction Basics (pg. 111) for binding instructions.

Bonus Table Runner

TABLE RUNNER SIZE
16" x 44"

BLOCK SIZE
12" finished

SUPPLY LIST
(5) 10" solid squares
1 yard background – includes
  sashing and border strips

BACKING
1 yard

BINDING
½ yard

SAMPLE QUILT
Kona Solids, 1178 Indigo, 355
Cayenne, 165 Ivy, 192 Mango, and
Essex Linen, Oyster E064-1268

1 cut

From the background fabric, cut:

- (1) 10" strip across the width of the fabric – Subcut the strip into (2) 10" squares. From the remainder of the strip, cut (4) 2½" x 20" strips. Subcut the strips into 2½" x 4½" rectangles. Each strip will yield 4 rectangles for a **total of 16.**

- (1) 4½" strip across the width of the fabric - Subcut the strip into (3) 4½" squares. Cut the remainder of the strip into (8) 2½" x 4½" rectangles. Stack these rectangles with the 16 you have already cut.

- (4) 2½" strips across the width of the fabric. Subcut 1 strip into (3) 2½" x 12½" rectangles. Set these aside for sashing. Cut another 2½" x 12½" rectangle from 1 remaining strip. Add it to the stack you set aside for sashing. Set aside the remaining background strips for the long border pieces.

2 sew

Refer to the Block Construction directions on page 44-45. **Make 3** blocks. Each block finishes at 12".

3 arrange and sew

Sew the 3 blocks together into a row. Begin the row with a 2½" x 12½" sashing rectangle and add a sashing rectangle between each block. End the row with a sashing rectangle.

Sew the 2 full remaining background 2½" x width of fabric strips together end-to-end, then add the remaining portion of the strip from which the 2½" x 12½" sashing rectangle was cut. Measure the table runner through the center and trim 2 strips to that measurement for the long top and bottom borders. The measurement should be approximately 44½". Cut 2 pieces that length. Sew 1 to the top of the runner and one to the bottom. Refer to Borders (pg. 111) in the Construction Basics, if necessary.

4 quilt and bind

Layer the table runner with batting and backing and quilt. After the quilting is complete, square up the table runner and trim away all excess batting and backing. Add binding to complete the table runner. See Construction Basics (pg. 111) for binding instructions.

snail trail

Kids have the most amazing questions. In my years teaching my children, I believe I've learned just as much from them as they have from me. I love the way their bright, young minds see the world. They ask about things like why the sky is blue, how fish breathe underwater, what light is made of, where dreams come from, and what's on the edge of the universe. The truth is, I often didn't know how to answer those insightful questions and so I had to be honest and tell them that I wasn't sure yet, but I would find out.

The seasons changed and the children grew, and one fall day while on a walk my youngest asked, "Why do the leaves change color?" I thought I knew the answer, but as I struggled to explain it using words like chlorophyll, I realized I needed more information. We finished our walk, gathering up the most beautiful leaves we could find so we could take a closer look at home. Then we set off to the library. It wasn't so easy then, we couldn't simply look up the answer on the internet. Together we went in search of the answer in the pages of a book.

For the tutorial and everything you need to make this quilt visit:
www.msqc.co/blockfall17

That morning the library was practically deserted. We searched through the shelves and found ourselves surrounded by a pile of books in the 580 section about "Plants, flowers, and trees." It felt cozy sitting there with open books on our laps, breathing in the scent of the yellowed pages. Soon we found our answer.

It turns out that trees aren't all green. The chlorophyll (I knew that part was right!) makes the leaves appear green. It's the food that trees live on and they make it with water, sugar, and sunlight. In the fall some plants stop making chlorophyll to prepare for the winter because there is less sunlight. It's their way of saving energy. When that happens, the true colors underneath the green come out—brilliant hues of red, orange, yellow, and even purple.

We pored over that book, learning about trees and how they make changes for each season. We were amazed at all the work that goes into the beautiful colors of fall. It was also a profound moment for me, sitting with this little one who wanted to know so many things about the world. I realized that we are always changing too.

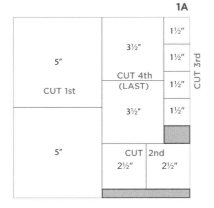

materials

QUILT SIZE
76" X 91"

BLOCK SIZE
7½" finished

QUILT TOP
1 package 10" print squares
1 package background 10" squares

INNER BORDER
¾ yard

BORDER
1½ yards

BINDING
¾ yard

BACKING
5½ yards – vertical seam(s)

SAMPLE QUILT
Aflutter by Elizabeth Isles
for Studio E

1 cut

To make the most of your fabric squares, refer to the diagram and cut the following pieces in the order given. Be sure to keep all matching prints together as you cut!

(2) 5" x 10" rectangles – subcut 1 rectangle into (2) 5" squares.

From the remaining rectangle, cut (1) 2½" x 5" rectangle horizontally – subcut the rectangle into (2) 2½" squares.

Cut (1) 1½" strip vertically from the remaining rectangle – subcut the strip into (4) 1½" squares.

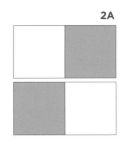

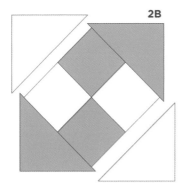

2B

Cut the remaining piece into (2) 3½″ squares. 1A

Set aside all 1½″ squares to use when making 4-patch units.

Cut each of the remaining squares from corner to corner once on the diagonal. Stack all triangles that have been cut the same size and use the same print together.

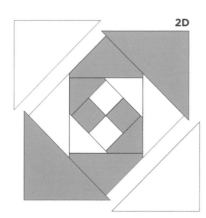

2C

2 block construction

Use matching prints when making the block.

Sew (4) 1½″ squares together as shown to make a 4-patch unit. 2A

Sew a print 2½″ triangle to opposite sides of the 4-patch. Then sew a background 2½″ triangle to the 2 remaining sides. 2B

Sew a print 3½″ triangle to opposite sides of the center unit. Add a background 3½″ triangle to the 2 remaining sides. 2C

Stitch a print 5″ triangle to opposite sides of the center unit. Add a background 5″ triangle to the 2 remaining sides of the center unit to complete the block. **Make 80 blocks** and square each to 8″. 2D

Block Size: 7½″ finished

3 arrange and sew

Lay out the blocks in rows. Each row is made up of 8 blocks and 10 rows are needed. After the blocks have been sewn into rows, press the seam allowances of the odd-numbered rows toward the right and the even-numbered rows toward the left to make the seams "nest."

Sew the rows together to complete the center of the quilt.

4 inner border

Cut (7) 2½″ strips across the width of the fabric. Sew the strips together end-to-end to make one long strip. Trim the borders from this strip.

Refer to Borders (pg. 111) in the Construction Basics to measure and cut the inner borders. The strips are approximately 75½″ for the sides and approximately 64½″ for the top and bottom.

5 outer border

Cut (8) 6½″ strips across the width of the fabric. Sew the strips together end-to-end to make one long strip. Trim the borders from this strip.

2D

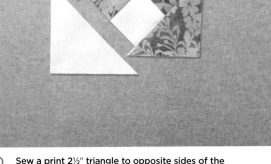

1 Sew (4) 1½" squares together as shown to make a 4-patch unit.

2 Sew a print 2½" triangle to opposite sides of the 4-patch. Then sew a background 2½" triangle to the 2 remaining sides.

3 Sew a print 3½" triangle to opposite sides of the center unit. Add a background 3½" triangle to the 2 remaining sides.

4 Stitch a print 5" triangle to opposite sides of the center unit. Add a background 5" triangle to the 2 remaining sides of the center unit to complete the block.

5 Make 80 blocks and square each to 8".

Refer to Borders (pg. 111) in the Construction Basics to measure and cut the outer borders. The strips are approximately 79½" for the sides and approximately 76½" for the top and bottom.

6 quilt and bind

Layer the quilt with batting and backing and quilt. After the quilting is complete, square up the quilt and trim away all excess batting and backing. Add binding to complete the quilt. See Construction Basics (pg. 111) for binding instructions.

stack & flip

I have some strong opinions about apples. There are over 7,500 varieties of apples grown all over the world, but of the ones that I'm familiar with, I can tell you exactly why I love them and what I like to use them for. I enjoy a sweet, tart Braeburn apple for eating, as well as a nice Fuji or a Pink Lady, also known as Cripps Pink. For pies, I am picky and like a firm apple that holds its shape like a Jonagold or the increasingly-popular Honeycrisp. Applesauce calls for the classic Golden Delicious. No matter which apple you pick, there's nothing like a delicious apple pie in the fall. My year just isn't complete without baking up a few.

I have the best recipe for apple pie filling and when I find a great deal on apples, I'll buy a few extra pounds and whip up a batch for canning. There's nothing better in the middle of winter when the snow is on the ground than pulling homemade apple pies out of the oven.

As my seven children have grown up and gotten married, I have been blessed with amazing daughters and sons-in-law. Sarah's husband, Seth, is the second oldest of 11 kids and that

For the tutorial and everything
you need to make this quilt visit:
www.msqc.co/blockfall17

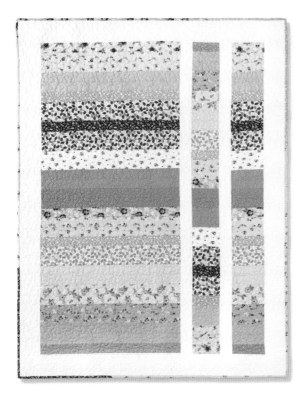

DOAN FAMILY

APPLE PIE FILLING

Put in stock pot and mix together everything except the lemon juice and apples.

4½ cup sugar
2 tsp cinnamon
½ tsp nutmeg
1 cup cornstarch

3 Tbs lemon juice
1 tsp salt
42 medium apples (⅓ bushel)

Add 10 cups water. Cook and stir until thickened and bubbly. Add 3 Tbs lemon juice and about 42 peeled, sliced, and cored apples (⅓ bushel). Put in jars filled just below the lip. Place in a hot water bath 20 mins. for quart size, 15 min for pints.

1 pint = 1 thick 8" pie or 1 thin 9" pie / 1 quart = 1 thick 9" pie or 1 thin 10" pie.

boy knows how to work. When I am in the middle of canning and he comes into the kitchen, he doesn't even ask, he just picks up a knife and starts peeling.

One day I got a call from Seth. He happened to be at the grocery store and saw that organic apples were on sale, so he called and asked if there was anything we could do with apples. I told him about my famous apple pie filling and asked him to get some apples for me. I didn't say how many pounds and imagined he'd just pick up a few. Well, he bought every apple they had!

That evening he came over with the load of apples, grabbed a pairing knife, and began to peel. I kindly thanked him for his efforts, and then I got out my apple peeler, screwed it onto the edge of the counter, plugged an apple into that contraption, and started turning the handle. He stood back in amazement, watching as the apple was peeled, cored, and sliced in less than a minute. He had never seen such a thing. The poor guy was completely prepared to peel all those apples by hand and so that apple peeler just made him giddy! That night we must have canned more than 50 quarts of apple pie filling. It was the best winter treat ever.

materials

QUILT SIZE
52" x 73" finished

QUILT TOP
1 roll of 2½" strips – includes binding
1¼ yards background fabric—
　includes border

BACKING
4½ yards - vertical seam(s)

SAMPLE QUILT
Sweet Prairie by Sedef Imer of
Down Grapevine Lane for Riley Blake

1 cut

From the background fabric, cut:

- (4) 3" strips across the width
  of the fabric – set aside to use
  as sashing strips. The remainder
  of the fabric will be used for the
  border.

2 sew

Select 32 strips from the roll and
arrange in a color order to your liking.
Sew the strips together along the
length.

After all the strips have been sewn
together, press all the seam allowances
in the same direction. Trim the selvages
from each end. In the process of
trimming, the large rectangle should be
squared up. **2A**

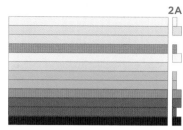

2A

+20 more strips

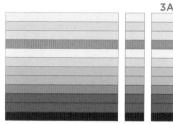

3A

+20 more strips

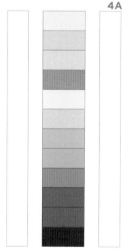

4A

+20 more strips

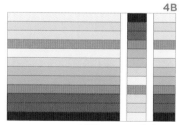

4B

+20 more strips

3 cut

From one end of the trimmed strips, cut (1) 7″ increment and (1) 6″ increment down the length of the strip set. **3A**

4 sew

Measure the length of the strip set. It should be approximately 64½″ long. Sew (2) 3″ sashing strips together end-to-end and trim to equal your measurement. **Make 2**. Pin a sashing strip to both sides of the 6″ increment.

Sew the sashing strips in place. **4A**

🐦 **NOTE:** *Pinning will keep the pieces in place and avoid any problem with stretching that might occur.*

Turn the sashed rectangle 180 degrees and, after pinning in place, sew the large strip set to the left and the 7″ increment to the right. Notice how the color order in the center is now reversed from the strip set on either side. **4B**

5 border

Cut (6) 5″ strips across the width of the fabric. Sew the strips together end-to-end to make one long strip. Trim the borders from this strip.

Refer to Borders (pg. 111) in the Construction Basics to measure and cut the borders. The strips are approximately 64½″ for the sides and approximately 52½″ for the top and bottom.

6 quilt and bind

Layer the quilt with batting and backing and quilt. After the quilting is complete, square up the quilt and trim away all excess batting and backing. Select 7 of the remaining strips from the roll and sew them together end-to-end to make the multi-colored binding. Add binding to complete the quilt. See Construction Basics (pg. 111) for complete binding instructions.

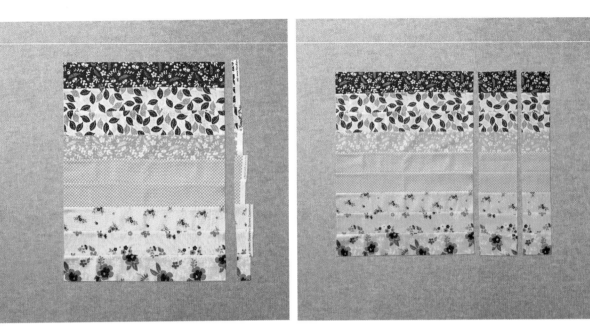

1 Select 32 strips from the roll of 2½″ strips. Sew the strips together along the length and trim the selvages from each end.

2 From one end of the trimmed strips, cut (1) 7″ increment and (1) 6″ increment down the length of the strip set.

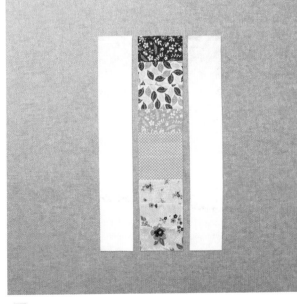

3 Sew a 3″ sashing strip to both sides of the 6″ increment.

4 Turn the sashed strip 180°. Sew the wider strip set to the left and the 7″ increment to the right.

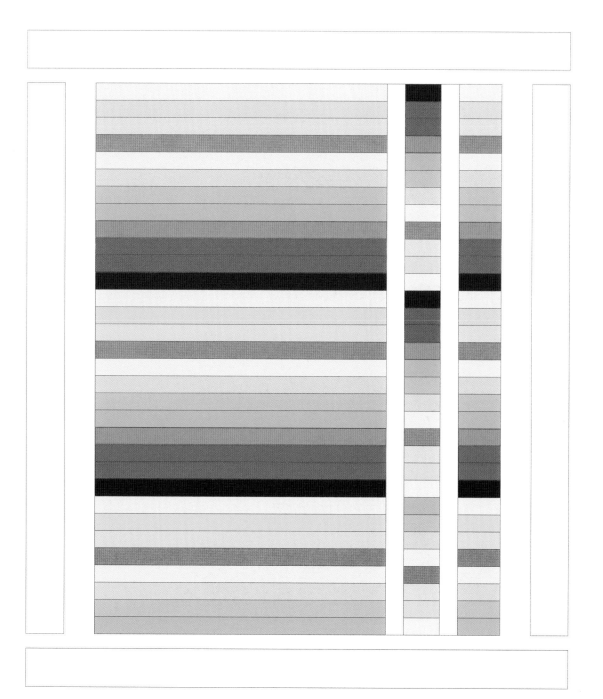

sweet
treats

At the end of a long, adventure-filled summer, it's hard to return to the grind of everyday life. Luckily, in the United States, we have Labor Day weekend, where we get the opportunity to enjoy one last hurrah before saying goodbye to summer.

My friend Louise has ten granddaughters, all close in age and the best of friends. Unfortunately, they're spread all across the state, so it can be hard to spend time together. Years ago, when the girls were young teenagers, Louise decided to host a girls-only weekend of quilting. She had already pieced together a quilt top, and she thought it would be fun to teach the girls to quilt the old-fashioned way.

When the girls arrived they came racing down the steps in a flurry of giggles. Louise showed them how to carefully tack the backing to her quilt frames. When all the fabric was smooth and taut, they rolled out a fluffy layer of batting and topped it off with her red, white, and blue churn dash quilt top.

Each girl was armed with a thimble and a silver needle. Louise demonstrated how to weave the needle up and down

For the tutorial and everything you need to make this quilt visit:
www.msqc.co/blockfall17

through the layers of fabric in order to make several stitches at once. She explained how to check for tangles on the underside of the quilt, and she patiently worked out tangles and knots. Before long, the girls were quilting up a storm, and as they stitched, they chattered like squirrels.

It got later and later, and pretty soon Louise said goodnight and went to bed. But still the girls quilted. They popped popcorn and snuck treats out of the candy jar. They watched classics like *State Fair* and *Seven Brides for Seven Brothers* and *Meet Me in St.*

Louis. By the time those girls finally climbed into their sleeping bags, the sun was about ready to rise.

The next morning they finished up the last few stitches, took the quilt off the frames, and began work on the binding. I'm sure you can imagine that with eleven sets of hands, it didn't take long to finish!

And so a new tradition was born. The girls are now grown with families of their own, but every year when Labor Day rolls around, they head to Louise's home for all-night quilting at Grandma's house!

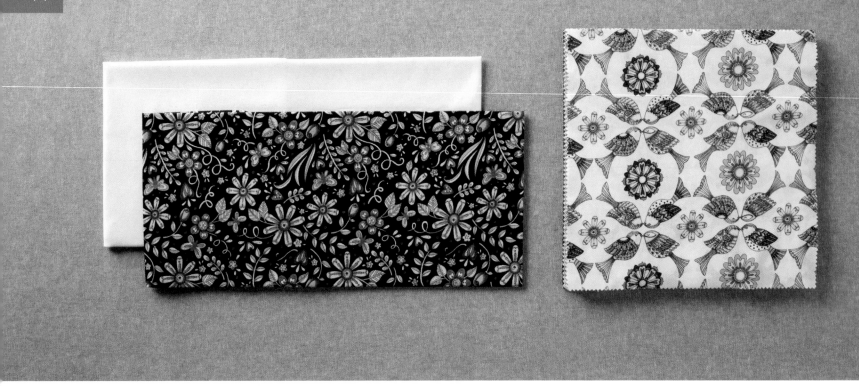

materials

QUILT SIZE
78" x 94" finished

BLOCK SIZE
16" finished

SUPPLIES
1 package of 10" print squares
1 package of 10" background squares

INNER BORDER
¾ yard

OUTER BORDER
1½ yards

BINDING
¾ yard

BACKING
2½ yards of 108" wide fabric

OTHER SUPPLIES
1 package Cake Mix - Recipe 1
papers by Miss Rosie's Quilt Co.
for Moda

SAMPLE QUILT
Lori's Art Garden by Lori Gardner
Woods for RJR Fabrics

1 layer and sew

Layer a print square with a background square with right sides facing and the lightest square on top. Pin a printed sheet from the package on top of the squares. Notice the star in the upper right corner that says, "Start." Adjust the stitch length on your sewing machine so you have about 12 stitches to the inch. Begin sewing on the dotted line at the starting point. Simply follow the directions of the arrow points and continue to sew. Each stitch line is marked in the order it's to be sewn.

After you have sewn on all the dotted stitch lines, cut on the solid lines. The first cut you make is clearly marked with an arrow pointing to the solid line and says, "Cut this line first." Be sure to cut on all the solid lines.

Remove the paper from each piece. You will have 1 large 8" finished half-square triangle and 4 smaller 4" finished half-square triangles. Open and press the seam allowances toward the darker fabric. One paper makes one-half of the block so you will need to follow the above directions and **make 2**.

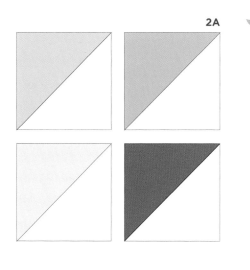

2A

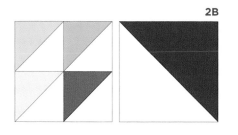

2B

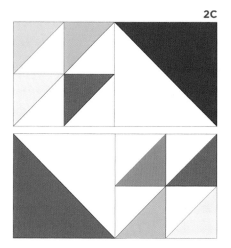

2C

🐦 **NOTE:** *If you want your quilt to have a scrappy look, mix up all the half-square triangles rather than trying to color-coordinate them.*

2 block construction

Sew 4 small half-square triangles together in a 4-patch layout. **Make 2** for each block. **2A**

Sew a set of half-square triangles to a large half-square triangle. **Make 2. 2B**

Sew the 2 sections together to complete the block. **Make 20** blocks. **2C**

Block Size: 16″ finished

3 arrange and sew

Arrange the blocks in rows of 4. When you are happy with the arrangement, sew the rows together. **Make 5** rows. Press the seam allowance of every other row in the opposite direction, odd rows toward the right and even rows toward the left. Sew the rows together to complete the center of the quilt.

4 inner border

Cut (8) 2½″ strips across the width of the fabric. Sew the strips together end-to-end to make one long strip. Trim the borders from this strip.

Refer to Borders (pg. 111) in the Construction Basics to measure and cut the inner borders. The strips are approximately 80½″ for the sides and approximately 68½″ for the top and bottom.

5 outer border

Cut (9) 5½″ strips across the width of the fabric. Sew the strips together end-to-end to make one long strip. Trim the borders from this strip.

Refer to Borders (pg. 111) in the Construction Basics to measure and cut the outer borders. The strips are approximately 84½″ for the sides and approximately 78½″ for the top and bottom.

6 quilt and bind

Layer the quilt with batting and backing and quilt. After the quilting is complete, square up the quilt and trim away all excess batting and backing. Add binding to complete the quilt. See Construction Basics (pg. 111) for binding instructions.

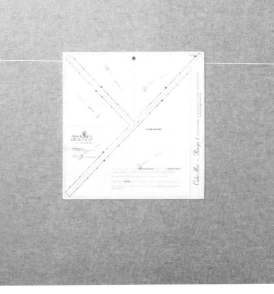

1 Select a package of Cake Mix Recipe 1 papers made by Miss Rosie's Quilt Co. for Moda.

2 Layer a background 10" square with a print 10" square. Pin the printed sheet on top of the squares and simply sew on the dotted stitch lines in the order given. Cut on the solid lines.

3 Remove the paper from the back and press the small half-square triangles open.

4 Stitch the 4 small half-square triangles together into a 4-patch unit. Sew the large half-square triangle to the 4-patch unit to complete one half of the block. Make 2.

5 Sew the 2 halves together to complete one block.

For the tutorial and everything you need to make this quilt visit: **www.msqc.co/blockfall17**

two step

There's something to be said for growing up in a small town. Here in the rural Midwest, kids know how to work, and many of them are milking cows and plowing fields well before they're old enough to drive a car. And after chores are done, they sure know how to have fun as well! During the summer, they build treehouses in their own backyards. They ride bikes for miles and miles just to buy an ice cold soda at the gas station. They splash into nearby swimming holes and soak up the golden yellow sun until suppertime.

At the end of a long, lazy summer vacation, kids in Hamilton are ready to head back to school. There are so many fun traditions that go along with this time of year, but I think my favorite is our annual "Drive Your Tractor to School Day," complete with parade.

If you've never been to a small-town parade, you are missing out. We all head downtown to set up chairs out in front of the quilt shops and restaurants. Townsfolk holler and cheer as kid-driven tractors of every shape and size rumble down the street, tossing candy as they go. You have to understand, most of these kids have grown up driving tractors. They know how to handle those tricky gear shifts and massive wheels, and it's such fun to show off in front of the whole town.

The tractors are as varied as the kids who drive them. I've seen everything from huge combines with six-foot-tall tires to adorable little mini tractors that could drive right through my front door. Kids who don't own tractors often join the parade on riding lawn mowers, and the littlest ones sit on the sidelines and collect candy like it's Halloween.

The tractor parade is a day I wait for all year long, and when it arrives, I just can't wipe the smile off my face. And if you are lucky enough to be in Hamilton for our favorite back-to-school tradition, I'm sure you will smile, too!

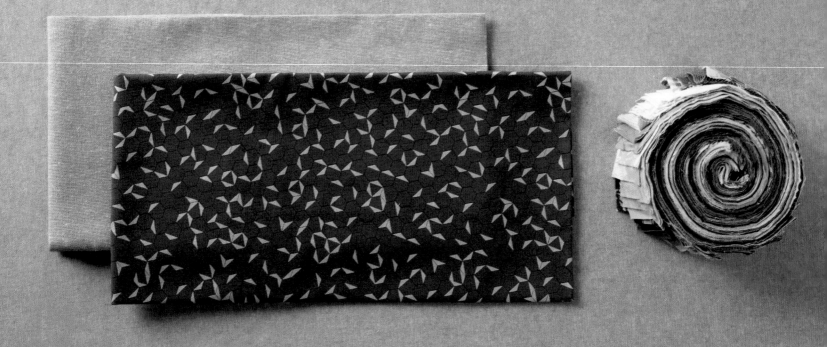

materials

QUILT SIZE
74½" X 83"

BLOCK SIZE
8½" finished

QUILT TOP
1 roll of 2½ print strips plus (2) 2½
    strips cut across the width of the
    fabric used for the outer border
1¾ yards background fabric—
    includes inner border

OUTER BORDER
1¾ yards

BINDING
¾ yard

BACKING
5¼ yards – vertical seam(s)

SAMPLE QUILT
Shimmer On by Jennifer Sampou for
Robert Kaufman

1 cut

From the background fabric, cut:

- (7) 5" strips across the width of
    the fabric – subcut each strip into
    (8) 5" squares for a **total of 56.**

Set the remainder of the fabric aside for
the inner border.

From the outer border fabric, cut:

- (2) 2½" strips across the width of
    the fabric and add them to the
    (40) 2½" strips from the roll. Set
    the remainder of the fabric aside
    for the border.

2A

3A

2 make strip sets

Sew (2) 2½ strips together along the long edges with right sides facing. Open and press the seam allowances toward the darker fabric. **Make 21.** 2A

Cut each of 7 strip sets into (8) 5" increments for a **total of 56.**

Cut each of the remaining 14 strip sets into (4) 9" increments for a **total of 56.**

3 block construction

Stitch (1) 5" strip set to one side of a 5" background square. 3A

Add (1) 9" strip set to the adjacent side as shown to complete the block. **Make 56.** 3B

Block Size: 8½" finished

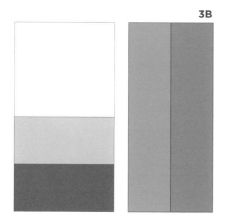

3B

4 arrange and sew

Lay out the blocks in rows. Each row is made up of 7 blocks and 8 rows are needed. Refer to the diagram on page 81 and notice how every other block is turned ¼ turn from the preceding block. After the blocks have been sewn into rows, press the seam allowances of the odd-numbered rows toward the right and the even-numbered rows toward the left to make the seams "nest."

Sew the rows together to complete the center of the quilt.

5 inner border

Cut (7) 2½" strips across the width of the fabric. Sew the strips together end-to-end to make one long strip. Trim the borders from this strip.

Refer to Borders (pg. 111) in the Construction Basics to measure and cut the inner borders. The strips are approximately 68½" for the sides and approximately 64" for the top and bottom.

6 outer border

Cut (8) 6" strips across the width of the fabric. Sew the strips together end-to-end to make one long strip. Trim the borders from this strip.

Refer to Borders (pg. 111) in the Construction Basics to measure and cut the outer borders. The strips are approximately 72½" for the sides and approximately 75" for the top and bottom.

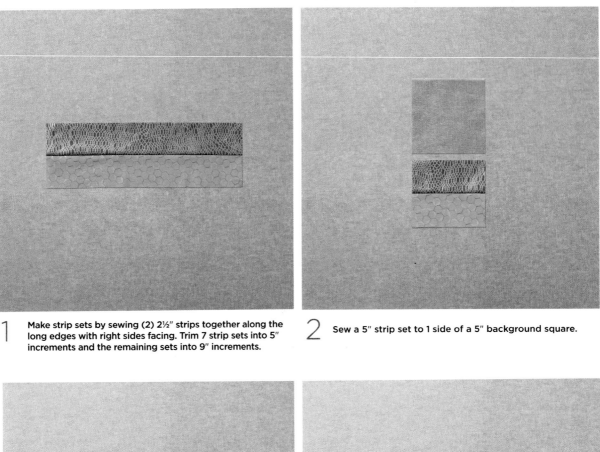

1 Make strip sets by sewing (2) 2½" strips together along the long edges with right sides facing. Trim 7 strip sets into 5" increments and the remaining sets into 9" increments.

2 Sew a 5" strip set to 1 side of a 5" background square.

3 Sew a 9" strip set to the right to complete the block.

4 Make 56 blocks.

7 quilt and bind

Layer the quilt with batting and backing and quilt. After the quilting is complete, square up the quilt and trim away all excess batting and backing. Add binding to complete the quilt. See Construction Basics (pg. 111) for binding instructions.

For the tutorial and everything you need to make this quilt visit:
www.msqc.co/blockfall17

wedge

Here in Hamilton, we're lucky to be surrounded by farms of all sorts. I love to watch the fields of wheat transform from delicate green sprouts to waving, golden stalks of grain. During the summer months, we have a wonderful farmers' market where you can get beautiful, fresh produce and other local goods.

At the end of the growing season, I'm sure that some farmers breathe a little sigh of relief. Their work isn't done, of course, but it may be a little less intense for a few weeks. I know of one West Coast farm where the real fun doesn't even begin until after the harvest is over.

This little farm has been owned by the same family for generations. I suppose every onion that has ever been eaten in that town was grown in that very soil. And every October they open the gates and invite the community to join in a fall festival.

When my friend Pat took her son, Benjamin, for a visit, he was in three-year-old heaven! Right off the bat they toured the fields in a trailer pulled by a big, green tractor. "Farmer Jim" pointed out watermelons, sunflowers, and, of course, those famous onions. They stopped alongside a field filled with pumpkins of every shape and size. Every child was invited to walk out into the field and pick a pumpkin to keep. Little Benji chose a small green variety that was covered in bumps. "It's a wicked witch jack o' lantern!" he told his mom.

The next stop was a large, open area that had been transformed into a farm-themed playground. Kids climbed up a mountain of straw bales and slid down the other side on a thick roll of plastic. They wandered through mazes cut into a dry cornfield. They bounced on the belly of a giant cow bounce house. There was so much to do, Benjamin's little body didn't know which way to run. Suddenly his eyes got big and he squealed, "Mama! A train!"

Sure enough, there was a little makeshift train pulling kids around an empty onion field. The "engine" was a small tractor, and the cars were made of old water barrels that had been cut and painted to look like pigs, chickens, and cows. It was a bumpy ride on that dry, old ground, and everywhere the train drove, it left a giant cloud of dust, but for Benjamin it was heaven.

At the end of the day, Pat and Benjamin left the farm exhausted but happy. Pat went home with a basket of squash, onions, and bell peppers from the produce stand at the entrance. Benjamin went home with his bumpy green pumpkin and the determination to become a train-driving farmer with a big green tractor. Thank goodness for farmers!

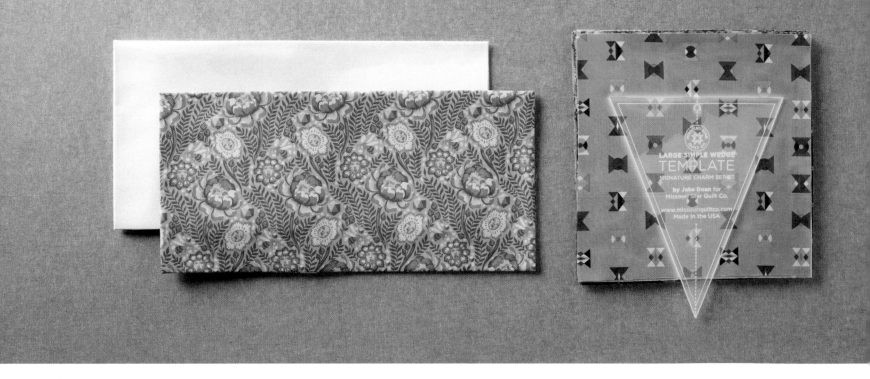

materials

QUILT SIZE
62" x 62" finished

BLOCK SIZE
16" finished

SUPPLIES
1 package 10" print squares
2 yards background – includes inner border

OUTER BORDER
1 yard

BINDING
¾ yard

BACKING
4 yards - vertical seam(s)

OTHER SUPPLIES
MSQC Large Simple Wedge template

SAMPLE QUILT
Spirit Animal by Tula Pink for Free Spirit Fabrics

1 cut

Select 18 of the 10" print squares. From each square, cut 2 wedges using the MSQC large simple wedge template. Set the rest of the squares aside for another project.

From the background fabric, cut:
(4) 9" strips across the width of the fabric - subcut each strip into 9 wedges using the template. Be sure to flip the template 180 degrees with each cut. A **total of 36** wedges are needed. **1A**

(3) 6" strips across the width of the fabric – subcut each strip into 6" squares. Each strip will yield 6 squares

1A

2A

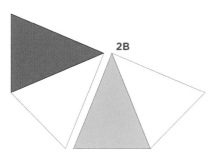

2B

and a **total of 18** are needed. Cut each square from corner to corner once on the diagonal to **make 36** triangles. Set aside for the moment.

Set the remainder of the background fabric aside for the inner border.

2 block construction

Pair a background wedge with a print wedge. Sew together using a ¼" seam allowance. **Make 4** pairs. 2A

Join 2 pairs to make one half of the block. **Make 2.** 2B

Sew the two halves together. 2C

Sew a background triangle to each background wedge in the block to make corners and complete the block. **Make 9** and square each block to 16½". 2D

Block Size: 16" finished

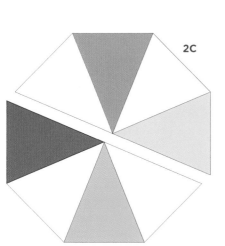

2C

3 arrange and sew

Lay out the blocks in rows. Each row is made up of 3 blocks and 3 rows are needed. After the blocks have been sewn into rows, press the seam allowances of the odd-numbered rows toward the right and the even-numbered rows toward the left to make the seams "nest."

Sew the rows together to complete the center of the quilt.

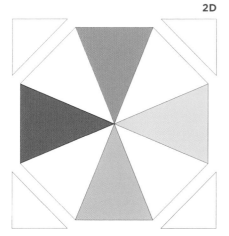

2D

4 inner border

Cut (6) 2½" strips across the width of the fabric. Sew the strips together end-to-end to make one long strip. Trim the borders from this strip.

Refer to Borders (pg. 111) in the Construction Basics to measure and cut the inner borders. The strips are approximately 48½" for the sides and approximately 52½" for the top and bottom.

5 outer border

Cut (6) 5½" strips across the width of the fabric. Sew the strips together end-to-end to make one long strip. Trim the borders from this strip.

Refer to Borders (pg. 111) in the Construction Basics to measure and cut the outer borders. The strips are approximately 52½" for the sides and approximately 62½" for the top and bottom.

6 quilt and bind

Layer the quilt with batting and backing and quilt. After the quilting is complete, square up the quilt and trim away all excess batting and backing. Add binding to complete the quilt. See Construction Basics (pg. 111) for binding instructions.

1   Cut 9″ strips across the width of the background fabric. Use the large simple wedge template to cut each strip into 9 wedges. Flip the template 180° with each cut to make the most of your fabric.

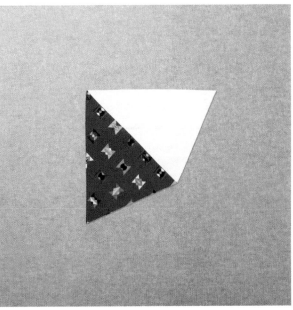

2   Pair a background wedge with a print wedge. Sew together using a ¼″ seam allowance. Make 4 pair.

3   Join 2 pairs to make one half of the block. Make 2.

4   Sew the two halves together.

5   Sew a background triangle to each background wedge in the block to make corners and complete the block.

6   Square each block to 16½″.

Irony: The Opposite of Wrinkly

You know you're a quilter when the ironing board is always set up, but you never iron clothes! Pressing is as much a part of quilting as stitching together beautifully patterned blocks. I learned early on in my quilting career that it was crucial to press seams before piecing the quilt top together or the result would be disappointing. At the very beginning, I'll admit, I was in a hurry; I wanted to see a quilt come together as quickly as possible without pausing to iron. After all, what could it hurt? Well, I soon found out how frustrating it is to try and nestle seams together and make points match. Quilting is an art and I've learned to enjoy each part of the process, including the ironing.

I'm choosy about my irons and I've even become a bit of a collector. You may have heard about my growing collection of toy sewing machines, but I'm also an avid iron enthusiast. I love adding to my collection of antique irons every time I visit a new town to teach at the local quilt guild. They are each so different, from a crimping iron to a dolphin-shaped sleeve iron. I even lugged home a huge tailor's iron that weighs almost 30 pounds! Delving into history and learning about the way things were gives me a greater appreciation for my life.

No one knows exactly when irons were invented, but in the Middle Ages blacksmiths began producing simple flat irons for use at home. These early irons were nothing more than a chunk of metal, pottery, or stone with a smooth base and a handle. Flat irons were also called "sad irons," sad meaning solid. They were placed in the fire to heat up and then used directly on cloth. Trying to avoid scorching was tough, not to mention the sheer weight of the iron. It gives a brand new meaning to pumping iron, doesn't it? It was a challenge to keep them heated for long and soon modifications were made to the original design. Box irons or charcoal irons were hollow inside and hot coals or heated slabs of metal were placed within and stayed hot for longer periods of time. Some irons were heated with kerosene, ethanol, whale oil, natural gas, or even gasoline. Can you imagine using a gas-powered iron?

Then, irons became electrified. In New York City in 1882, Henry W. Seeley invented the first safe electric iron. This new type of iron had a heating element that was controlled by thermostat, which made ironing much more adaptable and precise. After that, steam was added to the ironing process, making it even more efficient. Max Skolnik of Chicago invented the steam iron in 1934 and soon after, the Steam-O-Matic corporation began making these incredible irons, which gained widespread appeal in the 1940s and 50s.

Although the shape and purpose of the iron hasn't changed much, the mechanics of it have become much more advanced. Progressing from irons heated in fires to electric irons, now they have a variety of settings and features that allow for precise temperature control with different fabrics, water reservoirs for steam, retractable cords, nonstick coatings, automatic shutoff mechanisms, self-cleaning features, energy-saving modes, cordless models, and my favorite iron even lifts right off of the ironing board all by itself. It's amazing what this simple device has become and how its purpose has remained consistent. The next time you stop by an antique store or a garage sale, if you see an antique iron, give it a heft and thank your lucky stars for your iron at home. And most importantly, don't forget to press to the dark side!

Quilt Tales
- a quilt along story -

Have you ever wondered what stories a quilt might tell? Do you find yourself daydreaming, longing for a little adventure? Let yourself be transported to a place outside of time and reality, and get lost in a magical world we've created just for you. Our favorite fairy tales have inspired us to create a unique quilting experience called "Quilt Tales." Each issue of BLOCK Magazine this year will contain a new chapter in a story to complement a quilt pattern. Stitch along with us and let your imagination run free!

The Forest Bride
By Nichole Spravzoff

BLOCK FIVE
SNOWFALL

When Ingrid awoke, the whole world seemed quieter. The wind had died down. All was still. She peeped out through her curtains and saw that there was a fresh blanket of snow covering everything, including the trees. It made the scene look so peaceful, despite the damage from the storm. Although it was late in the year for a snowfall, it wasn't unheard of. Clearing the fallen trees would have to wait until the snow melted again. She supposed it was just her rotten luck, complicating her life and making her change her plans once more. Well, if the trees had to wait, she would settle in and work on the projects that had piled up over the past couple weeks. There was a stack of towels to embroider for a young bride's dowry, a pair of trousers with holes in the knees that needed patches, and a torn quilt she had just begun repairing. It was beautiful, even after years of use. She touched the border gently, running her fingers over the triangles that mimicked the shape of geese flying south for the winter. It had been made years earlier by her mother. She would know those tiny, neat stitches anywhere.

The week passed by slowly as the snow receded while Ingrid stitched calmly by the fire. The quilt came back together, piece by piece, and she felt soothed by the change of pace. After so many things happening so quickly, the solitude was pleasant, but her thoughts kept returning to the afternoon she spent in Skogsmark with Gustav. He was different than she'd ever imagined. And then there was his confession. Somewhere inside herself she had found the strength to forgive him. It still made her tear up when she thought of it, but it also made her feel something else. She found herself wondering why he had held her hand. The touch of his work-hardened hand was not unwelcome, it was warm and comforting. It felt familiar to her, like her father's hands hoisting her up to sit on his neck while she laughed and gazed at the tops of the trees.

When the remaining snow revealed patches of dark earth and bright blue lady's thimbles growing through the frost, Ingrid went into town to hire woodcutters to remove the fallen trees around her cabin. The best place to find them would be at the pub, taking a midday break sipping aquavit. They huddled around the scrubbed wooden counter, drinking intently and talking idly to each other in between sips. Ingrid slipped inside without a sound and went unnoticed. Before she could ask her favor, she heard a piece of gossip sail through the air and land with a thump before her.

"That Hansson boy is getting married soon, you know," one man said.

"Pretty girl too," another added.

"He'll be coming into his own, handling his father's affairs now."

"About time too!"

They all chattered on, laughing and commenting on the latest happenings around the village. Ingrid cleared her throat and stepped up to the counter. "I'll have a cup of tea," she murmured to the barkeep. Her thoughts were now swirling around the gossip and everything else faded into the background. She had to ask.

"Are you talking about Karl Hansson?" She asked a steely-looking man sitting next to her.

"Mmhmm," he muttered in the affirmative.

"And he'll be taking over his father's business now?" She ventured.

"I suppose so," he answered shortly.

Another man cut in, "Didn't his brother come after you?" He cocked an eyebrow and a presumptuous grin spread across his face.

Ingrid's face went scarlet. She turned away from his blunt question and sipped her tea with a shaking hand. Apparently the word had spread. After a moment, she gathered up her courage and addressed the quieter man sitting next to her.

"Sir, I would like to ask for some assistance," she said.

"How may I be of help?" He looked up at her with genuine concern.

"During the storm a few large trees fell near my home. One is right in front of my door. I need some help clearing them," she explained.

"We'll send over some boys to take care of it as soon as we

can," he said deliberately, as if already considering the resources needed for the job.

"Thank you, sir," she nodded to him and left her half-empty teacup on the counter, still bristling at the unexpected question about Gustav.

Ingrid returned home and began her chores, which was a challenge without access to the front door. She crawled back inside and began sewing as she waited for help to arrive. Soon she heard the sound of hoofbeats and a wagon came into view with Karl at the reins and Gustav riding alongside him. She set down her needlework and went over to the window, mouth agape. Of all the people to send. She shook her head.

They set to work without a word from her, removing the smaller branches from the fallen tree in front of her door first and then, starting at the top, dividing the entire length of the tree into sections with a two-man crosscut saw. It would be impossible to cut through the trunk right in front of her door, so they attached it to a cart pulled by a horse which allowed them to drag the tree away from the house and continue to chop it up for firewood. Ingrid had left them to their task, content with the familiar sounds of chopping and sawing that filled the air.

Then, without warning, a large tree branch splintered and fell to the forest floor with a sharp crack. The horse whinnied. Immediately after, a man cried out sharply. Ingrid lept to her feet

and practically jumped through the window at the sound, not knowing that the tree in front of her door was already gone. As she got to her feet she surveyed the scene quickly and saw Gustav crying in pain. He lay crumpled at the side of the horse, who was still rearing up. Karl had the reins in his hand, trying to calm the horse. Watching the scrambling hooves carefully, Ingrid threw herself onto Gustav and rolled him over, away from the spooked horse. As she moved his body with the same effort as a large sack of flour, he groaned in pain.

"Where are you hurt?" She asked, searching for the injury.

He gritted his teeth and said, "It's my foot."

She looked down at his foot and saw that it was hanging at an odd angle. It made her feel ill. "I'll help you. You'll be okay," she assured him, trying not to cry or be sick.

Karl shouted to them, "I'm going to town to get the doctor!" He handily unhooked the wagon from the horse, jumped into the saddle and was gone within minutes.

Gustav's breathing became shallow and his teeth chattered. "I'm cold," he said.

"I'll be right back," she whispered. Ingrid whipped open the front door now that it was clear of the fallen tree and grabbed her mother's quilt and a pair of scissors. She wrapped the quilt around Gustav and tested his forehead with her wrist. Then she took a small piece of wood and propped up his injured leg. He cried out in pain. "I'm sorry. It should help," she said softly.

"Ughhh," he let out a muffled sigh.

"What happened?" She asked, trying to get him to talk.

"It fell ... the branch. Then the horse ..." he shivered and continued, "threw me off ... and my foot ..."

While he talked, Ingrid carefully sliced open his trouser leg with her scissors and saw that his ankle was bleeding. "I need to bandage your foot. Just wait." She went back inside, found her scrap bag and brought it back out with her. There were long pieces of muslin and tufts of wool inside. Those would do. Trying to remove his boot proved too painful, so she found two short sticks, placed them on either side of his leg, padded his ankle with the wool, and wound the pieces of fabric tightly around them and the boot to keep everything in place. When she was finished he was still moaning quietly to himself, but the bleeding was staunched and the foot was stable.

She said nothing more, but sat silently next to him, occasionally replacing the damp piece of fabric on his forehead. Otto even sensed the seriousness of the situation and positioned himself next to Gustav with his muzzle on Gustav's arm. Time passed, and Gustav's breathing became more regular. Then she heard the sound of a horse and buggy in the distance. "The doctor's almost here, Gustav." She assured him.

His lips parted, but he said nothing.

When the doctor arrived, he commended Ingrid on her quick thinking while Karl stood to the side, looking contrite. The doctor also noted that her choice to splint the leg was insightful and helped the swelling to go down, but the foot was definitely broken. They gently hoisted Gustav onto Ingrid's bed and the doctor administered to him there.

"It'd be best to keep him here overnight," he remarked. "If that's okay with you, Ingrid."

She nodded and said little while the doctor worked to carefully remove the boot and examine Gustav's foot.

"I'll send over a bonesetter as soon as possible," the doctor said lightly, as if he were sending over a tin of biscuits. "The blacksmith does a fine job." He deftly rewrapped Gustav's foot, snapped his large, black bag shut and left in a hurry along with Karl.

"I'm sorry this happened to you," she said to Gustav, unsure if he had heard her or not.

He opened his eyes partially and looked at her as if she were standing afar off. "You saved me," he said.

"No, I didn't," she insisted.

He fixed his gaze on her and said with as much strength as he could muster, "Yes, you did."

to be continued...

block of the month

Flying Geese
Block Size: 4" x 8" finished

SUPPLY LIST
(16) 10" white squares
(16) 10" blue squares

draw, layer, and sew
Draw a line from corner to corner twice on the diagonal on the reverse side of each white square. Place a white square atop a blue square with right sides facing. Sew ¼" on either side of each of the drawn lines.

Cut the sewn squares in half vertically and horizontally. Then cut on the drawn lines. Open each section to reveal a half-square triangle unit and square each to 4½". Each set of sewn squares will yield 8 half-square triangles. A **total of 128** are needed.

block construction
Sew 2 half-square triangles together to make 1 flying geese block. **Make 64.**

Sew 14 flying geese together as shown. Make 2 rows like this and sew 1 to either side of the center of the quilt. Be aware that the geese are flying toward the top on the right and toward the bottom on the left.

Sew 18 flying geese together into a row. Notice how the first 2 geese are turned. Make 2 rows and sew 1 to the top and 1 to the bottom. Again, be aware of the direction the geese are flying.

This quilt top is not finished yet. It will be continued in the next issue when everything comes together.

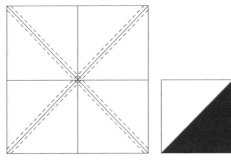

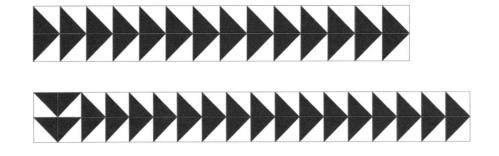

disappearing pinwheel twist

QUILT SIZE
81" x 99"

BLOCK SIZE
11" x 12" finished

QUILT TOP
1 package print 10" squares
1 package background 10" squares

INNER BORDER
¾ yard

OUTER BORDER
1¾ yards

BINDING
¾ yard

BACKING
2½ yards 108" wide

SAMPLE QUILT
Shibori II by Debbie Maddy of Tiori
Designs for Moda Fabrics

QUILTING PATTERN
Dragonflies

ONLINE TUTORIALS
msqc.co/blockfall17

PATTERN
pg. 8

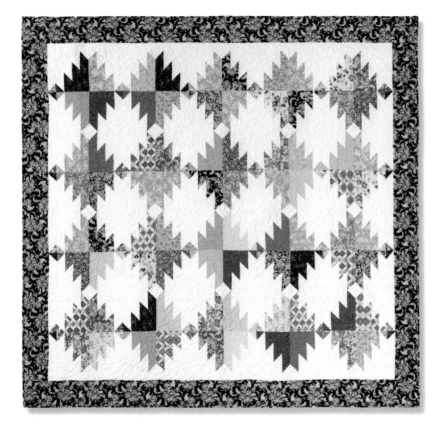

grand adventures

QUILT SIZE
90¾" x 87¾"

BLOCK SIZE
15" x 18" finished

QUILT TOP
1 package 10" print squares
1 package 10" background squares

BORDER
¾ yard

OUTER BORDER
1¾ yards

BINDING
1 yard

BACKING
2¾ yards 108" wide

SAMPLE QUILT
Charming by Gerri Robinson
of Planted Seed Designs for
Penny Rose Fabrics

QUILTING PATTERN
Drop of Paisley

ONLINE TUTORIALS
msqc.co/blockfall17

PATTERN
pg. 16

herringbone

QUILT SIZE
86" x 98"

BLOCK SIZE
6" x 12" finished

SUPPLIES
1 package 10" print squares
1 package 10" background squares

INNER BORDER
¾ yard

OUTER BORDER
1½ yards

BINDING
1 yard

BACKING
8 yards - horizontal seam(s)

SAMPLE QUILT
Safari Party by Melissa Mortenson
for Riley Blake Designs

QUILTING PATTERN
Loops & Swirls

ONLINE TUTORIALS
msqc.co/blockfall17

PATTERN
pg. 24

pecking order

QUILT SIZE
66" X 70½"

BLOCK SIZE
4½" finished

QUILT TOP
1 pack 5" solid squares
4 packs 5" print background squares

BORDER
1½ yards

BINDING
¾ yard

BACKING
4¼ yards – horizontal seam(s)

SAMPLE QUILT
Penned Pals by Ann Kelle for Robert Kaufman

QUILTING PATTERN
Paws 2

ONLINE TUTORIALS
msqc.co/blockfall17

PATTERN
pg. 32

pony
express

QUILT SIZE
83" X 83"

BLOCK SIZE
12" finished

QUILT TOP
1 package 10" print squares
4½ yards background fabric

BORDER
1½ yards

BINDING
¾ yard

BACKING
2¾ yards 108" wide fabric

SAMPLE QUILT
Chicken Scratch by Kaye England
for Wilmington Prints

QUILTING PATTERN
Posies

ONLINE TUTORIALS
msqc.co/blockfall17

PATTERN
pg. 40

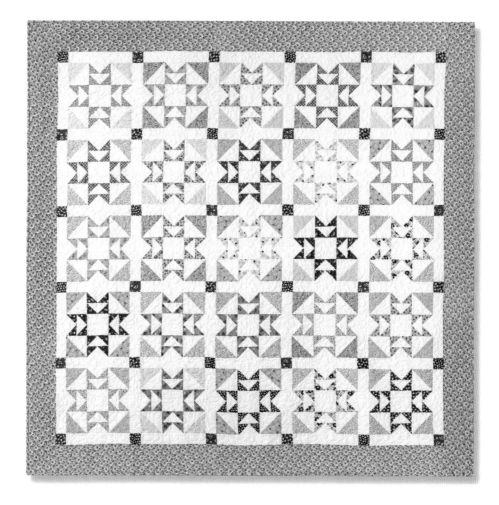

pony express table runner

TABLE RUNNER SIZE
16" x 44"

BLOCK SIZE
12" finished

SUPPLY LIST
(5) 10" solid squares
1 yard background – includes
    sashing and border strips

BACKING
1 yard

BINDING
½ yard

SAMPLE QUILT
Kona Solids, 1178 Indigo, 355
Cayenne, 165 Ivy, 192 Mango, and
Essex Linen, Oyster E064-1268

QUILTING PATTERN
Free motion

ONLINE TUTORIALS
msqc.co/blockfall17

PATTERN
pg. 48

snail
trail

QUILT SIZE
76" X 91"

BLOCK SIZE
7½" finished

QUILT TOP
1 package 10" print squares
1 package background 10" squares

INNER BORDER
¾ yard

BORDER
1½ yards

BINDING
¾ yard

BACKING
5½ yards – vertical seam(s)

SAMPLE QUILT
Aflutter by Elizabeth Isles
for Studio E

QUILTING PATTERN
Champagne Bubbles

ONLINE TUTORIALS
msqc.co/blockfall17

PATTERN
pg. 50

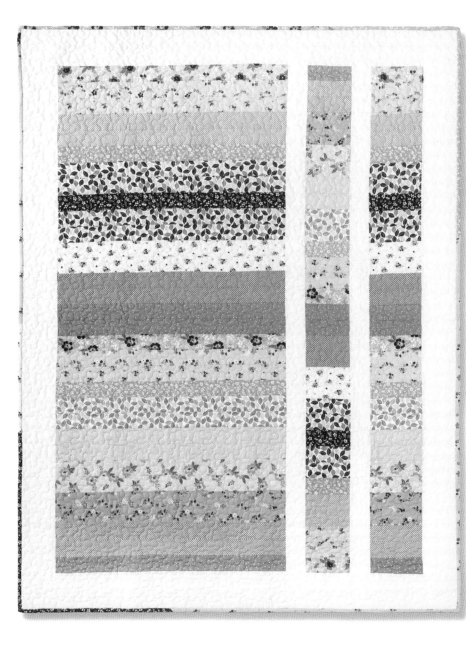

stack & flip

QUILT SIZE
52" x 73" finished

QUILT TOP
1 roll of 2½" strips – includes binding
1¼ yards background fabric –
   includes border

BACKING
4½ yards - vertical seam(s)

SAMPLE QUILT
Sweet Prairie by Sedef Imer of
Down Grapevine Lane for Riley Blake

QUILTING PATTERN
Cotton Candy

ONLINE TUTORIALS
msqc.co/blockfall17

PATTERN
pg. 58

sweet
treats

QUILT SIZE
78" x 94" finished

BLOCK SIZE
16" finished

SUPPLIES
1 package of 10" print squares
1 package of 10" background squares

INNER BORDER
¾ yard

OUTER BORDER
1½ yards

BINDING
¾ yard

BACKING
2½ yards of 108" wide fabric

OTHER SUPPLIES
1 package Cake Mix - Recipe 1
papers by Miss Rosie's Quilt Co.
for Moda

SAMPLE QUILT
Lori's Art Garden by Lori Gardner
Woods for RJR Fabrics

QUILTING PATTERN
Flutterby

ONLINE TUTORIALS
msqc.co/blockfall17

PATTERN
pg. 66

two step

QUILT SIZE
74½" X 83"

BLOCK SIZE
8½" finished

QUILT TOP
1 roll of 2½ print strips plus (2) 2½
    strips cut across the width of the
    fabric used for the outer border
1¾ yards background fabric –
    includes inner border

OUTER BORDER
1¾ yards

BINDING
¾ yard

BACKING
5¼ yards – vertical seam(s)

SAMPLE QUILT
Shimmer On by Jennifer Sampou
for Robert Kaufman

QUILTING PATTERN
Champagne Bubbles

ONLINE TUTORIALS
msqc.co/blockfall17

PATTERN
pg. 74

wedge diamond

QUILT SIZE
62" x 62" finished

BLOCK SIZE
16" finished

SUPPLIES
1 package 10" print squares
2 yards background – includes inner
   border

OUTER BORDER
1 yard

BINDING
¾ yard

BACKING
4 yards - vertical seam(s)

OTHER SUPPLIES
MSQC Large Simple Wedge template

SAMPLE QUILT
Spirit Animal by Tula Pink for
Free Spirit Fabrics

QUILTING PATTERN
Flower Swirls

ONLINE TUTORIALS
msqc.co/blockfall17

PATTERN
pg. 82

construction basics

general quilting

- All seams are ¼" inch unless directions specify differently.
- Cutting instructions are given at the point when cutting is required.
- Precuts are not prewashed; therefore do not prewash other fabrics in the project.
- All strips are cut width of fabric.
- Remove all selvages.

press seams

- Use a steam iron on the cotton setting.
- Press the seam just as it was sewn right sides together. This "sets" the seam.
- With dark fabric on top, lift the dark fabric and press back.
- The seam allowance is pressed toward the dark side. Some patterns may direct otherwise for certain situations.
- Follow pressing arrows in the diagrams when indicated.
- Press toward borders. Pieced borders may demand otherwise.
- Press diagonal seams open on binding to reduce bulk.

borders

- Always measure the quilt top 3 times before cutting borders.
- Start measuring about 4" in from each side and through the center vertically.
- Take the average of those 3 measurements.
- Cut 2 border strips to that size. Piece strips together if needed.
- Attach one to either side of the quilt.

- Position the border fabric on top as you sew. The feed dogs can act like rufflers. Having the border on top will prevent waviness and keep the quilt straight.
- Repeat this process for the top and bottom borders, measuring the width 3 times.
- Include the newly attached side borders in your measurements.
- Press toward the borders.

binding

find a video tutorial at: www.msqc.co/006

- Use 2½" strips for binding.
- Sew strips end-to-end into one long strip with diagonal seams, aka the plus sign method (next). Press seams open.
- Fold in half lengthwise wrong sides together and press.
- The entire length should equal the outside dimension of the quilt plus 15" - 20."

plus sign method

- Lay one strip across the other as if to make a plus sign right sides together.
- Sew from top inside to bottom outside corners crossing the intersections of fabric as you sew.
  Trim excess to ¼" seam allowance.
- Press seam open.

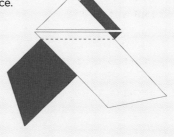

find a video tutorial at: www.msqc.co/001

attach binding

- Match raw edges of folded binding to the quilt top edge.
- Leave a 10" tail at the beginning.
- Use a ¼" seam allowance.
- Start in the middle of a long straight side.

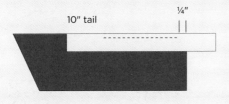

10" tail   ¼"

miter corners

- Stop sewing ¼" before the corner.
- Move the quilt out from under the presser foot.
- Clip the threads.
- Flip the binding up at a 90° angle to the edge just sewn.
- Fold the binding down along the next side to be sewn, aligning raw edges.
- The fold will lie along the edge just completed.
- Begin sewing on the fold.

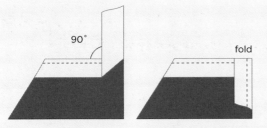

90°   fold

close binding

MSQC recommends The Binding Tool from TQM Products to finish binding perfectly every time.

- Stop sewing when you have 12" left to reach the start.
- Where the binding tails come together, trim excess leaving only 2½" of overlap.
- It helps to pin or clip the quilt together at the two points where the binding starts and stops. This takes the pressure off of the binding tails while you work.
- Use the plus sign method to sew the two binding ends together, except this time when making the plus sign, match the edges. Using a pencil, mark your sewing line because you won't be able to see where the corners intersect. Sew across.

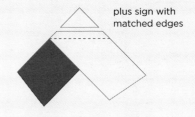

plus sign with matched edges

- Trim off excess; press seam open.
- Fold in half wrong sides together, and align all raw edges to the quilt top.
- Sew this last binding section to the quilt. Press.
- Turn the folded edge of the binding around to the back of the quilt and tack into place with an invisible stitch or machine stitch if you wish.